I0568213

Learn to Write and Spell -

Homophones

The Danger Twins Writing Series

ISBN PAPERBACK: 978-1-956547-10-8

Book design by Anne Lusher

Published by Unplanned Books, LLC.

UNPLANNED BOOKS

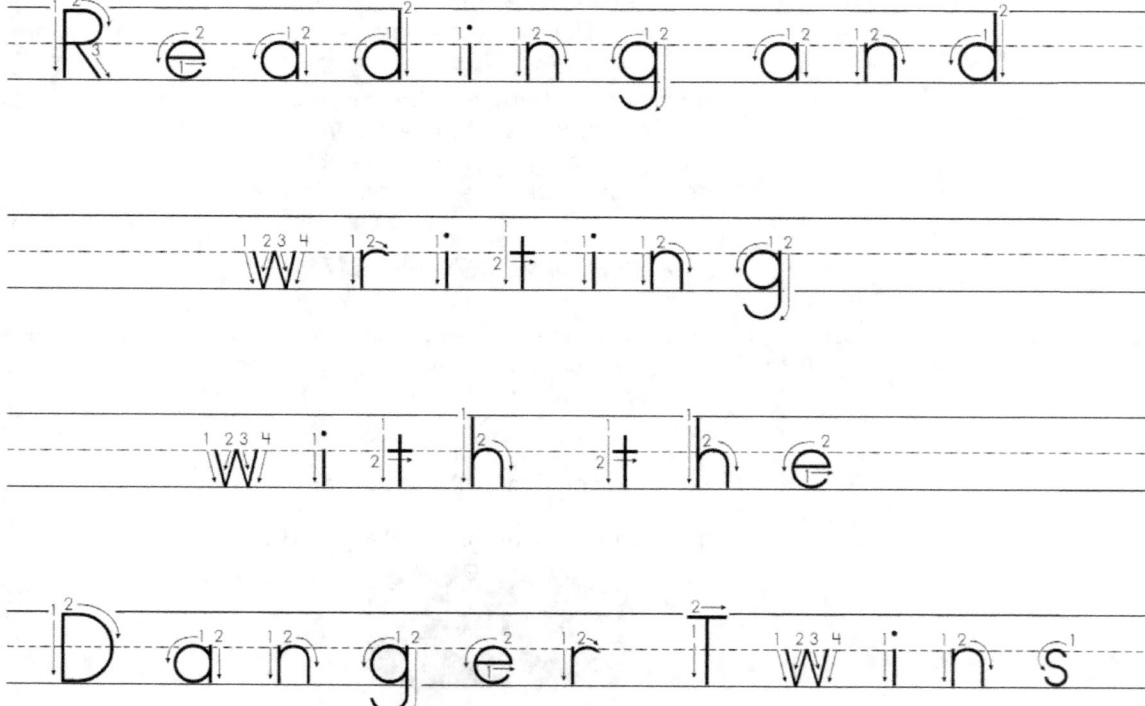

Reading and writing with the Danger Twins

HOMOPHONES

Homophones sound similar,
but have different meanings

Write down what you think the correct
homophone is for each word below.

1. reign

2. bye

3. grate

4. weak

5. many

6. steal

HOMOPHONES

Sean Danger has the answers!
The correct homophones pairs are below.
Trace each word and say it aloud.

1. rain   (reign)

2. by or buy   (bye)

3. great   (grate)

4. week   (weak)

5. merry   (marry)

6. steel   (steal)

4

THE DANGER TWINS

Trace and write the letters below in cursive.

a a a a a a a

a a a a a a a

a a

a a a a a a

a a a a a a

a a

THE DANGER TWINS

Trace and write the words below in cursive.

ad   or   add

ad ad ad ad

The newspaper showed the ad.

ad   or   add

add add add add

I can add two plus nine.

THE DANGER TWINS

Trace and write the words below in cursive.

ant   or   aunt

ant ant ant ant

The ant was on the food.

ant   or   aunt

aunt aunt aunt aunt

Aunt Kim came to visit us.

THE DANGER TWINS

Trace and write the words below in cursive.

ale   or   ail

ale ale ale ale

He opened the bottle of ale.

ale   or   ail

ail ail ail ail

I felt sick and ail all day.

THE DANGER TWINS

Trace and write the letters below in cursive.

b *b* *b* *b* *b* *b* *b*

b *b* *b* *b* *b* *b* *b*

b *b*

B *B* *B* *B* *B* *B*

B *B* *B* *B* *B* *B*

B *B*

B

b

THE DANGER TWINS

Trace and write the words below in cursive.

bear   or   bare

bear bear bear bear

The bear took all of my food.

bear   or   bare

bare bare bare bare

Your skin is bare in the bath.

THE DANGER TWINS

B

b

Trace and write the words below in cursive.

bee   or   be

bee bee bee bee

The bee was on the honeypot.

bee   or   be

be be be be

I want to be a doctor.

11

THE DANGER TWINS

Trace and write the words below in cursive.

berry   or   bury

berry berry berry berry

The berry is purple and ripe.

berry   or   bury

bury bury bury bury

I can bury it in the sand.

THE DANGER TWINS

Read each sentence and circle the correct homophone.

1   This insect has six legs and is an ____.   AUNT or ANT

2   I was stung on my arm by the ____.   BEE or BE

3   I can ____ two + two.   AD or ADD

4   The baby ate the juicy ____.   BERRY or BURY

5   In the woods we saw a grizzly ____.   BARE or BEAR

6   The newspaper posted my ____.   AD or ADD

7   We need to ____ on time today.   BE or BEE

8   The man drank ____ from the bottle.   AIL or ALE

9   We want to ____ the treasure chest.   BERRY or BURY

10   I spoke to ____ Kim on the phone.   ANT or AUNT

11   My skin is not covered and is ____.   BEAR or BARE

12   Today I feel sick and ____.   AIL or ALE

13

THE DANGER TWINS

a *B*

Each sentence below contains new bonus words.
Read each sentence and circle the correct homophone.

1   The bride and groom approached the ____.   ALTAR or ALTER

2   We perform in a rock and roll ____.   BAND or BANNED

3   Please ____ all of the numbers together.   AD or ADD

4   The girl read her fictional story ____.   ALLOWED or ALOUD

5   The boy can play the guitar and ____.   BASE or BASS

6   A doctor came to her ____.   AID or AIDE

7   We need an extra loaf of ____.   BREAD or BRED

8   The bride walked down the ____.   AISLE or I'll

9   I have ____ looking for a treasure chest.   BEEN or BIN

10   They plan to ____ a new house.   BILLED or BUILD

11   The doctor made us wait and I was ____.   BOARD or BORED

12   The girl slipped and landed on her ____.   BUT or BUTT

14

WRITING WITH THE DANGER TWINS

The Danger Twins
love puzzles.
Use the letters in the word,
HOMOPHONES
and write as many words
that you can unscramble.

phone   shop

shone

C

THE DANGER TWINS

Trace and write the letters below in cursive.

C

c c c c c c c

c c c c c c c

c c

c c c c c

c c c c c

C C

THE DANGER TWINS

Trace and write the words below in cursive.

C   c

chili   or   chilly

chili chili chili chili

The chili is hot and spicy.

chili   or   chilly

chilly chilly chilly chilly

Wear a hat if you are chilly.

C

THE DANGER TWINS

Trace and write the words below in cursive.

c

cereal   or   serial

cereal cereal cereal cereal

I poured milk on my cereal.

cereal   or   serial

serial serial serial serial

The serial number is ten digits.

THE DANGER TWINS

Trace and write the words below in cursive.

capitol or capital

capitol capitol capitol capitol

The capitol has marble steps.

capitol or capital

capital capital capital capital

We wrote in capital letters.

THE DANGER TWINS

Trace and write the letters below in cursive.

d d d d d d d d

d d d d d d d d

d d

D D D D D D

D D D D D D

D D

THE DANGER TWINS

Trace and write the words below in cursive.

deer   or   dear

deer deer deer deer

The deer ran away quickly.

deer   or   dear

dear dear dear dear

She is a dear friend of ours.

THE DANGER TWINS

D

d

Trace and write the words below in cursive.

dye   or   die

dye dye dye dye

The red dye is a chemical.

dye   or   die

die die die die

The goldfish did not die.

THE DANGER TWINS

Trace and write the words below in cursive.

doe   or   dough

doe doe doe doe

A doe lives in the forest.

doe   or   dough

dough dough dough dough

I made a bowl of cookie dough.

THE DANGER TWINS

C · D

Read each sentence and circle the correct homophone.

1. He ordered a large bowl of ____. CHILI or CHILLY

2. My mom rolled out the cookie ____. DOE or DOUGH

3. We toured the U.S. ____. CAPITOL or CAPITAL

4. I mixed in a dark blue ____. DYE or DIE

5. She opened the box of breakfast ____. CEREAL or SERIAL

6. I saw five ____ in our yard. DEER or DEAR

7. Every winter I am cold and ____. CHILI or CHILLY

8. Our pet is alive and did not ____. DYE or DIE

9. We startled the ____ in the forest. DOE or DOUGH

10. Every ____ number is sixteen digits. CEREAL or SERIAL

11. Start the letter with ____ Santa. DEER or DEAR

12. They have raised a lot of ____. CAPITOL or CAPITAL

THE DANGER TWINS

Each sentence below contains new bonus words.
Read each sentence and circle the correct homophone.

C

D

1   Please paint the walls and the ____.   CEILING or SEALING

2   The sand is hot in the ____.   DESERT or DESSERT

3   A penny is worth one ____ .   CENT or SCENT

4   Please ____ your chores after school.   DEW or DO

5   The girl was able to ____ her dress.   CHEWS or CHOOSE

6   The crowd had a lot of loud ____.   CHANTS or CHANCE

7   The man tried to ____ the paper target.   CHUTE or SHOOT

8   He ____ just in time.   DUCKED or DUCT

9   The crab has sharp ____.   CLAUSE or CLAWS

10 We splashed around in the ____.   CREAK or CREEK

11 The car was banged up with many ____.   DENSE or DENTS

12 She ____ food with her mouth shut.   CHEWS or CHOOSE

THE DANGER TWINS

Trace and write the letters below in cursive.

26

THE DANGER TWINS

Trace and write the words below in cursive.

eight   *or*   *ate*

eight eight eight eight

We have eight cousins our age.

8

eight   *or*   *ate*

ate ate ate ate

We just ate dinner.

THE DANGER TWINS

Trace and write the words below in cursive.

eye   or   I

eye eye eye eye

Her eye color is blue.

eye   or   I

I I I I

I really like this workbook.

THE DANGER TWINS

Trace and write the words below in cursive.

ewe   or   you

ewe ewe ewe ewe

The ewe is a sheep.

ewe   or   you

you you you you

Both of you were helpful.

F # THE DANGER TWINS

Trace and write the letters below in cursive.

THE DANGER TWINS

Trace and write the words below in cursive.

flower   or   flour

flower flower flower flower

The girl sniffed the flower.

flower   or   flour

flour flour flour flour

I added flour to make dough.

THE DANGER TWINS

F

f

Trace and write the words below in cursive.

four   or   for

four four four four

There are four seasons per year.

four   or   for

for for for for

You can ask for directions.

THE DANGER TWINS

Trace and write the words below in cursive.

fare   or   fair

fare fare fare fare

The man paid the subway fare.

fare   or   fair

fair fair fair fair

Her fair skin burns easily.

THE DANGER TWINS

Read each sentence and circle the correct homophone.

1   We counted five, six, seven and ____.   EIGHT or ATE

2   Next school year, I will be in grade ____.   FOUR or FOR

3   The ____ is a big animal.   EWE or YOU

4   She did not cut the ____ stem.   FLOWER or FLOUR

5   Tonight we ____ dinner early.   EIGHT or ATE

6   The train ____ is expensive.   FARE or FAIR

7   Wow, ____ did not know that.   EYE or I

8   Vegetables are good ____ you.   FOUR or FOR

9   I would like ____ to attend.   EWE or YOU

10   Follow the rules to be ____.   FARE or FAIR

11   The girl held ____ balloons.   EIGHT or ATE

12   Please bring a five pound bag of ____.   FLOWER or FLOUR

THE DANGER TWINS

Each sentence below contains new bonus words.
Read each sentence and circle the correct homophone.

1   Ten students were sick with the ____.   FLEW or FLU

2   It was ____ her turn to leave.   FINALLY or FINELY

3   The detective went over the ____.   FAX or FACTS

4   She jumped up and onto her ____.   FEAT or FEET

5   The basketball player committed a ____.   FOUL or FOWL

6   The number remaining is just a ____   FEW or PHEW

7   I could not see the color of her ____.   EYES or AYES

8   There is a lot of treasure to ____.   FIND or FINED

9   A message was made by the town ____.   FRIAR or FRYER

10 The boy was dizzy and ____.   FAZED or PHASED

11 Animals have a lot of warm ____.   FIR or FUR

12 The dog had a ____.   FLEA or FLEE

35

THE DANGER TWINS

Trace and write the letters below in cursive.

THE DANGER TWINS

Trace and write the words below in cursive.

gate   or   gait

gate gate gate gate

A gate blocks the road.

gate   or   gait

gait gait gait gait

The horse trotted with a gait.

THE DANGER TWINS

Trace and write the words below in cursive.

gourd   or   gored

gourd gourd gourd gourd

The garden had a big gourd.

gourd   or   gored

gored gored gored gored

The bison gored the deer.

THE DANGER TWINS

$\mathscr{G}$ g

Trace and write the words below in cursive.

graham   *or*   *gram*

graham graham graham graham

The girl ate a graham cracker

graham   *or*   *gram*

gram gram gram gram

A gram is a unit of weight

THE DANGER TWINS

Trace and write the letters below in cursive.

h   *h*

h h h h h h h

h h h h h h h

h h

H H H H H H H

H H H H H H H

H H

THE DANGER TWINS

Trace and write the words below in cursive.

hole   or   whole

hole hole hole hole

The boy jumped over the hole.

hole   or   whole

whole whole whole whole

We ate the whole cake.

THE DANGER TWINS

Trace and write the words below in cursive.

heel   or   heal

heel heel heel heel

He scraped the heel of his foot.

heel   or   heal

heal heal heal heal

I could try to heal the dog.

THE DANGER TWINS

Trace and write the words below in cursive.

hour   or   our

hour hour hour hour

An hour is sixty minutes.

hour   or   our

our our our our

That cat is our favorite pet.

THE DANGER TWINS

Trace and write the letters below in cursive.

i i i i i i

i i i i i i

i i

l l l l l l

l l l l l l

l l

THE DANGER TWINS`

Trace and write the words below in cursive.

I

i

inn   or   in

inn inn inn inn

The inn is similar to a hotel.

inn   or   in

in in in in

We walked in the park

THE DANGER TWINS

Read each sentence and circle the correct homophone.

1   We stopped at the tall iron ____.   GATE or GAIT

2   We cut open the delicious ____.   GOURD or GORED

3   The toddler ate a ____ cracker.   GRAHAM or GRAM

4   They almost fell into the ____.   HOLE or WHOLE

5   The deep cut on my finger will not ____.   HEEL or HEAL

6   Sixty minutes is equal to one ____.   HOUR or OUR

7   The motel is just like the ____.   INN or IN

8   One ____ is a small measurement.   GRAHAM or GRAM

9   My new shoe scrapped my ____.   HEEL or HEAL

10   The puppy is ____ pet.   HOUR or OUR

11   We will not jump ____ the pool.   INN or IN

12   We should share the ____ dessert.   HOLE or WHOLE

THE DANGER TWINS

Each sentence below contains new bonus words.
Read each sentence and circle the correct homophone.

1   We need to find an electrician to ____.   HIGHER or HIRE

2   Another word for a rabbit is a ____.   HAIR or HARE

3   I am going to be in the fourth ____.   GRADE or GRAYED

4   My car was running and was left to ____.   IDLE or IDOL

5   She enjoys riding a ____.   HOARSE or HORSE

6   Everyone walked into the reception ____.   HALL or HAUL

7   That was something I should have ____.   GUESSED or GUEST

8   We all need ____ to breath.   HEIR or AIR

9   Please stop talking so you can ____.   HEAR or HERE

10 I saw a 9-foot American ____.   GATOR or GAITER

11 The patient will ____ to wait.   HALVE or HAVE

12 I believe her score was ____.   HIGHER or HIRE

THE DANGER TWINS

J

Trace and write the letters below in cursive.

j j j j j j j

j j j j j j j

j j

J J J J J J

J J J J J J

J J

THE DANGER TWINS`

Trace and write the words below in cursive.

jewel or joule

jewel jewel jewel jewel

A thief stole the jewel.

jewel or joule

joule joule joule joule

Joule is a unit of energy.

THE DANGER TWINS

Trace and write the words below in cursive.

jam   or   jamb

jam jam jam jam

The lady put jam on her toast.

jam   or   jamb

jamb jamb jamb jamb

The door jamb was stuck.

THE DANGER TWINS

Trace and write the letters below in cursive.

𝓀 𝓀 𝓀 𝓀 𝓀 𝓀 𝓀

𝓀 𝓀 𝓀 𝓀 𝓀 𝓀 𝓀

𝓀 𝓀

𝒦 𝒦 𝒦 𝒦 𝒦 𝒦

𝒦 𝒦 𝒦 𝒦 𝒦 𝒦

𝒦 𝒦

THE DANGER TWINS`

K   *k*

Trace and write the words below in cursive.

knot   or   not

knot knot knot knot

He tied the rope into a knot.

knot   or   not

not not not not

I ordered juice, not milk.

THE DANGER TWINS

K   k

Trace and write the words below in cursive.

knight   or   night

knight knight knight knight

A knight wore a suit of armor.

knight   or   night

night night night night

The sky is dark at night.

53

THE DANGER TWINS

K

k

Trace and write the words below in cursive.

kernel   or   colonel

kernel kernel kernel kernel

I ate the popcorn kernel.

kernel   or   colonel

colonel colonel colonel colonel

He has the rank of colonel.

THE DANGER TWINS

Read each sentence and circle the correct homophone.

$\mathcal{J}$

1   The green ____ really sparkles.   JEWEL or JOULE

2   She made a jar of strawberry ____.   JAM or JAMB

3   The dog will ____ go inside.   KNOT or NOT

4   He was promoted to the rank of ____.   KERNEL or COLONEL

5   The armor suit is worn by the ____.   KNIGHT or NIGHT

6   Please tie the rope into a ____.   KNOT or NOT

7   We measured the ____ level.   JEWEL or JOULE

8   The door was broken on the ____.   JAM or JAMB

9   We stayed awake all ____.   KNIGHT or NIGHT

10 I heard the popcorn ____ pop.   KERNEL or COLONEL

11 The sky is dark at ____.   KNIGHT or NIGHT

12 Please do ____ mess up your bedroom.   KNOT or NOT

THE DANGER TWINS

Each sentence below contains new bonus words.
Read each sentence and circle the correct homophone.

1   His backyard has a large ____ pond.   KOI or COY

2   She was sick and had a stuffy ____.   KNOWS or NOSE

3   He did not answer yes or ____.   KNOW or NO

4   I look like my parents because of our ____.   JEANS or GENES

5   The quick response was said in ____.   JEST or GEST

6   That gold that was used was 14 ____.   KARAT or CARROT

7   He response was vague and ____.   KOI or COY

8   Before entering, we should ____.   KNOCK or NOCK

9   He ____ how to speak six languages.   KNOWS or NOSE

10 I am wearing my favorite pair of ____.   JEANS or GENES

11 The bunny was eating an orange ____.   KARAT or CARROT

12 Good question, but I really don't ____ .   KNOW or NO

THE DANGER TWINS

Trace and write the letters below in cursive.

ℓ ℓ ℓ ℓ ℓ ℓ ℓ

ℓ ℓ ℓ ℓ ℓ ℓ ℓ

ℓ ℓ

ℒ ℒ ℒ ℒ ℒ ℒ

ℒ ℒ ℒ ℒ ℒ ℒ

ℒ ℒ

THE DANGER TWINS'

Trace and write the words below in cursive.

lynx   or   links

lynx lynx lynx lynx

The lynx was ready to pounce.

lynx   or   links

links links links links

We play golf on the links.

THE DANGER TWINS

Trace and write the words below in cursive.

leak   or   leek

leak leak leak leak

The old pipe began to leak.

leak   or   leek

leek leek leek leek

I put a leek on my salad.

THE DANGER TWINS

Trace and write the words below in cursive.

lei   or   lay

lei lei lei lei

I placed a lei around her neck.

lei   or   lay

lay lay lay lay

The rug will lay on the floor.

THE DANGER TWINS

Trace and write the letters below in cursive.

𝓂   𝓂   𝓂   𝓂   𝓂   𝓂   𝓂

𝓂   𝓂   𝓂   𝓂   𝓂   𝓂   𝓂

𝓂   𝓂

𝓂   𝓂   𝓂   𝓂   𝓂   𝓂

𝓂   𝓂   𝓂   𝓂   𝓂   𝓂

𝓂   𝓂

THE DANGER TWINS

Trace and write the words below in cursive.

mail   or   male

mail mail mail mail

A package arrived in the mail.

mail   or   male

male male male male

The boy is also a male.

THE DANGER TWINS

Trace and write the words below in cursive.

moose or mousse

moose moose moose moose

The moose is a tall animal.

moose or mousse

mousse mousse mousse mousse

We made chocolate mousse.

M   # THE DANGER TWINS   *m*

Trace and write the words below in cursive.

maid   or   made

maid   maid   maid   maid

The maid had cleaning supplies

maid   or   made

made made made made

I made a batch of cookies.

THE DANGER TWINS

Trace and write the letters below in cursive.

n n n n n n n

n n n n n n n

n n

N N N N N N

N N N N N N

N N

THE DANGER TWINS

Trace and write the words below in cursive.

new   or   knew

new new new new

The store has new products.

NEW

new   or   knew

knew knew knew knew

I knew about the party.

THE DANGER TWINS

Trace and write the words below in cursive.

naval   or   navel

naval   naval   naval   naval

The naval ship was out to sea.

naval   or   navel

navel   navel   navel   navel

A navel is the center point.

THE DANGER TWINS

Read each sentence and circle the correct homophone.

L   *n*

1   Her parents bought her a ____ shirt.   KNEW or NEW

2   We saw a very tall ____.   MOOSE or MOUSSE

3   At the zoo we saw a ____.   LYNX or LINKS

4   He commanded the ____ vessel.   NAVAL or NAVEL

5   I enjoy opening the ____.   MAIL or MALE

6   The room was cleaned by the ____.   MADE or MAID

7   The bathtub seems to have a ____.   LEAK or LEEK

8   I want to ____ down and nap.   LEI or LAY

9   I will make ____ as a side dish.   MOOSE or MOUSSE

10 He used the ____ locker room.   MAIL or MALE

11 We ____ an ice sculpture.   MADE or MAID

12 He ____ we would get in trouble.   KNEW or NEW

THE DANGER TWINS

Each sentence below contains new bonus words.
Read each sentence and circle the correct homophone.

1   The boy is able to swim ten ____.   LAPS or LAPSE

2   I am glad we were able to finally ____.   MEAT or MEET

3   The teacher started the math ____.   LESSON or LESSEN

4   He did not know that you would ____.   MIND or MINED

5   I could see a small ray of ____.   LIGHT or LITE

6   The answer is ____ of the above.   NONE or NUN

7   The animal disappeared into the ____.   MISSED or MIST

8   The thief made off with a bag of ____.   LUTE or LOOT

9   I really ____ a nap today.   NEED or KNEAD

10 A monster once swam in the ____.   LOCH or LOCK

11 She ____ a wooden sculpture.   MADE or MAID

12 Do not let the dogs get ____.   LOOSE or LUCE

69

THE DANGER TWINS

Trace and write the letters below in cursive.

THE DANGER TWINS

Trace and write the words below in cursive.

oar   or   or

oar oar oar oar

An oar helps us move the boat.

oar   or   or

or or or or

You may have one or two.

THE DANGER TWINS

Trace and write the words below in cursive.

one   or   won

one one one one

I have one blue race car.

one   or   won

won won won won

My blue car won the race.

THE DANGER TWINS

Trace and write the letters below in cursive.

p p p p p p p

p p p p p p p

p p

p p p p p p

p p p p p p

p p

THE DANGER TWINS

Trace and write the words below in cursive.

pear   or   pair

pear pear pear pear

The pear was ripe and juicy.

pear   or   pair

pair pair pair pair

I own a pair of skates.

p

THE DANGER TWINS

Trace and write the words below in cursive.

p

plane   or   plain

plane plane plane plane

The plane just landed.

plane   or   plain

plain plain plain plain

My bagel was plain to eat.

THE DANGER TWINS

Trace and write the letters below in cursive.

q q q q q q q

q q q q q q q

q q

2 2 2 2 2 2

2 2 2 2 2 2

2 2

THE DANGER TWINS

$\mathscr{Q}$

q

Trace and write the words below in cursive.

quarts   or   quartz

quarts quarts quarts quarts

I made ten quarts of lemonade.

1 QUART
2 PINTS
4 CUPS
32 OUNCES
950 ML

quarts   or   quartz

quartz quartz quartz quartz

We found a piece of quartz.

Trace and write the words below in cursive.

Q *q*

queue   or   cue

queue queue queue queue

I stood in line, in the queue.

queue   or   cue

cue cue cue cue

I use my cue in billiards.

THE DANGER TWINS

Trace and write the letters below in cursive.

r r r r r r r

r r r r r r r

r r

R R R R R R

R R R R R R

R R

THE DANGER TWINS

Trace and write the words below in cursive.

ring   or   wring

ring ring ring ring

The lady wore a wedding ring.

ring   or   wring

wring wring wring wring

Wring water from the towel.

THE DANGER TWINS

Trace and write the words below in cursive.

road   or   rode

road road road road

The car traveled down the road.

road   or   rode

rode rode rode rode

The cowboy rode his horse.

THE DANGER TWINS

Trace and write the words below in cursive.

rose   *or*   *rows*

rose   *rose*   *rose*   *rose*

A rose is a pretty flower.

rose   *or*   *rows*

rows   *rows*   *rows*   *rows*

I sat in one of the empty rows.

THE DANGER TWINS

Read each sentence and circle the correct homophone.

1. She easily ____ the math competition.   ONE or WON

2. There is a long ____ of people waiting.   QUEUE or CUE

3. I am learning how to fly a ____.   PLANE or PLAIN

4. My favorite fruit is a juicy ____.   PEAR or PAIR

5. Please help make two ____ of iced tea.   QUARTS or QUARTZ

6. The red ____ has thorns.   ROSE or ROWS

7. The bride is wearing a wedding ____.   RING or WRING

8. He drove his antique car down the ____.   ROAD or RODE

9. To make the canoe move, use an ____.   OAR or OR

10. This sandwich tastes really ____.   PLANE or PLAIN

11. She needed a new ____ of shoes.   PEAR or PAIR

12. The movie theater has ____ of seating.   ROSE or ROWS

THE DANGER TWINS

O   *R*

Each sentence below contains new bonus words.
Read each sentence and circle the correct homophone.

1   I found the missing puzzle ____.   PEACE or PIECE

2   I do not know how long it will ____.   RAIN or REIGN

3   The library book is ____.   OVERDO or OVERDUE

4   I ____ my favorite book.   READ or RED

5   Add one can of tomato ____.   PACED or PASTE

6   He needs a pair of dice to ____.   ROLE or ROLL

7   A girl carried the water ____.   PAIL or PALE

8   The fireman slid down the ____.   PULL or POLE

9   The king's son was born a ____.   PRINTS or PRINCE

10   My favorite type of bread is ____.   RYE or WRY

11   Please ____ a glass of milk.   POUR or POOR

12   He drove his car along the assigned ____.   ROOT or ROUTE

THE DANGER TWINS

Trace and write the letters below in cursive.

THE DANGER TWINS

Trace and write the words below in cursive.

sail   or   sale

sail sail sail sail

The ship set sail today.

sail   or   sale

sale sale sale sale

My favorite dress is on sale.

THE DANGER TWINS

Trace and write the words below in cursive.

sun or son

sun sun sun sun

The sun brightens the sky.

sun or son

son son son son

That boy is her oldest son.

THE DANGER TWINS

Trace and write the words below in cursive.

shoe or shoo

shoe shoe shoe shoe

The boy tried on a new shoe.

shoe or shoo

shoo shoo shoo shoo

I tried to shoo away the bird.

THE DANGER TWINS

Trace and write the letters below in cursive.

t t t t t t t

t t t t t t t

t t

$\mathcal{T}$ $\mathcal{T}$ $\mathcal{T}$ $\mathcal{T}$ $\mathcal{T}$ $\mathcal{T}$

$\mathcal{T}$ $\mathcal{T}$ $\mathcal{T}$ $\mathcal{T}$ $\mathcal{T}$ $\mathcal{T}$

$\mathcal{T}$ $\mathcal{T}$

THE DANGER TWINS

Trace and write the words below in cursive.

tail   or   tale

tail tail tail tail

My dog wagged his tail.

tail   or   tale

tale tale tale tale

Someone told me a tale.

THE DANGER TWINS

Trace and write the words below in cursive.

toe   or   tow

toe   toe   toe   toe

She stubbed her toe.

toe   or   tow

tow   tow   tow   tow

The car needed a tow.

THE DANGER TWINS

Trace and write the words below in cursive.

two   or   too

two   two   two   two

Those two girls are twins.

2

two   or   too

too   too   too   too

I want to go too, but not now.

THE DANGER TWINS

Read each sentence and circle the correct homophone.

1   I can touch my big ____.   TOW or TOE

2   They are her daughter and her ____.   SUN or SON

3   You can go to the party, ____.   TWO or TOO

4   I tried on both a brown and black ____.   SHOE or SHOO

5   The boat left port and began to ____.   SAIL or SALE

6   The dog has a long ____.   TAIL or TALE

7   The truck is broken and needs a ____.   TOW or TOE

8   Never stare directly at the ____.   SUN or SON

9   Countdown four, three, ____ and one.   TWO or TOO

10   We would like to hear a scary ____.   TAIL or TALE

11   The store is having a big ____.   SAIL or SALE

12   Please try to ____ away the bugs.   SHOE or SHOO

THE DANGER TWINS

Each sentence below contains new bonus words.
Read each sentence and circle the correct homophone.

$\mathcal{S}$ $\mathcal{T}$

1   Everyone ordered a T-bone ____.   STEAK or STAKE

2   I will order a glass of iced ____.   TEA or TEE

3   In the back of the pond there is a ____.   TOAD or TOWED

4   She had a ____ in her eye.   TEAR or TIER

5   They performed in the final ____.   SCENE or SEEN

6   We camped outside in ____.   TENSE or TENTS

7   The ship went out to ____.   SEA or SEE

8   The final score was ____.   TIDE or TIED

9   The man was in the wine ____.   SELLER or CELLAR

10 The lid for the jar will not ____.   TIGHTEN or TITAN

11 The exhausted mom simply ____.   SIDE or SIGHED

12 Do not bully or ____.   TEAS or TEASE

94

U # THE DANGER TWINS *u*

Trace and write the letters below in cursive.

u u u u u u u u

u u u u u u u u

u u

U U U U U U U

U U U U U U U

U U

THE DANGER TWINS

Trace and write the words below in cursive.

urn   or   earn

urn urn urn urn

The items are now in the urn.

urn   or   earn

earn earn earn earn

I was able to earn ten dollars.

U *u*

Trace and write the words below in cursive.

unreel   or   unreal

unreel unreel unreel unreel

The film began to unreel.

unreel   or   unreal

unreal unreal unreal unreal

That was an unreal experience.

THE DANGER TWINS

Trace and write the letters below in cursive.

u u u u u u u

u u u u u u u

u u

v v v v v v

v v v v v v

v v

THE DANGER TWINS

Trace and write the words below in cursive.

veil   or   vale

veil   veil   veil   veil

The bride wore a wedding veil.

veil   or   vale

vale   vale   vale   vale

The vale is like a valley.

THE DANGER TWINS

Trace and write the words below in cursive.

$\mathcal{V}$ $\mathcal{v}$

Venus   or   venous

Venus Venus Venus Venus

Venus is in our solar system.

Venus   or   venous

venous venous venous venous

My arm was venous.

THE DANGER TWINS

Trace and write the letters below in cursive.

THE DANGER TWINS

Trace and write the words below in cursive.

whale   *or*   *wail*

whale whale whale whale

The whale is in the ocean.

whale   *or*   *wail*

wail wail wail wail

I heard the boy wail in pain.

THE DANGER TWINS

Trace and write the words below in cursive.

wood   or   would

wood wood wood wood

We moved the wood pile.

wood   or   would

would would would would

I would attend that school.

THE DANGER TWINS

Trace and write the words below in cursive.

witch or which

witch witch witch witch

The witch is a main character.

witch or which

which which which which

Pick which toy you want.

THE DANGER TWINS

Trace and write the letters below in cursive.

x x x x x x x

x x x x x x x

x x

X X X X X X

X X X X X X

X X

X *x*

Trace and write the words below in cursive.

ax   or   acts

ax   ax   ax   ax

The lumberjack used an ax.

ax   or   acts

acts   acts   acts   acts

The clown acts silly.

THE DANGER TWINS

Trace and write the letters below in cursive.

y y y y y y y

y y y y y y y

y y

Y Y Y Y Y Y

Y Y Y Y Y Y

Y Y

THE DANGER TWINS

Trace and write the words below in cursive.

yolk   or   yoke

yolk   yolk   yolk   yolk

I see the egg yolk.

yolk   or   yoke

yoke   yoke   yoke   yoke

The yoke secures the animals.

THE DANGER TWINS

Trace and write the letters below in cursive.

THE DANGER TWINS

Trace and write the words below in cursive.

zero   or   xero

zero zero zero zero

Multiply by zero to get zero.

zero   or   xero

xero xero xero xero

A common prefix is xero.

THE DANGER TWINS

Read each sentence and circle the correct homophone.

1   The men chopped enough ____.   WOOD or WOULD

2   There is no limit on what you can ____.   URN or EARN

3   The ____ character scared the children.   WITCH or WHICH

4   I like the number ____.   ZERO or XERO

5   The ____ splashes water with his flipper.   WHALE or WAIL

6   The ____ was heavy and sharp.   AX or ACTS

7   Crack open the egg ____.   YOLK or YOKE

8   The entire roll began to ____.   UNREEL or UNREAL

9   She ____ like to go to that movie.   WOOD or WOULD

10   I do not know ____ way to go.   WITCH or WHICH

11   The bride wore a lace ____.   VEIL or VALE

12   Multiply twenty and ____.   ZERO or XERO

THE DANGER TWINS

Each sentence below contains new bonus words.
Read each sentence and circle the correct homophone.

1   I am able to ____ the mess he made.   UNDO or UNDUE

2   The soldier went off to ____.   WAR or WORE

3   My temperature will ____ by a few degrees.   VARY or VERY

4   I know how much I ____.   WAY or WEIGH

5   The surfer caught a big ____.   WAVE or WAIVE

6   The clothes look old and ____.   WARN or WORN

7   The scientist only had one ____ left.   VIAL or VILE

8   He was sick, and felt ____.   WEEK or WEAK

9   Do not ____ natural resources.   WAIST or WASTE

10 I am only a ____ bit hungry.   WE or WEE

11 The children did not want to ____.   WAIT or WEIGHT

12 I certainly hope my answer is ____.   WRITE or RIGHT

ANSWERS FROM THE DANGER TWINS

The Danger Twins have the answer keys!

Page 13	Page 14	Page 24	Page 25	Page 34
1 ANT	1 ALTAR	1 CHILI	1 CEILING	1 EIGHT
2 BEE	2 BAND	2 DOUGH	2 DESERT	2 FOUR
3 ADD	3 ADD	3 CAPITOL	3 CENT	3 EWE
4 BERRY	4 ALOUD	4 DYE	4 DO	4 FLOWER
5 BEAR	5 BASS	5 CEREAL	5 CHOOSE	5 ATE
6 AD	6 AID	6 DEER	6 CHANTS	6 FARE
7 BE	7 BREAD	7 CHILLY	7 SHOOT	7 I
8 ALE	8 AISLE	8 DIE	8 DUCKED	8 FOR
9 BURY	9 BEEN	9 DOE	9 CLAWS	9 YOU
10 AUNT	10 BUILD	10 SERIAL	10 CREEK	10 FAIR
11 BARE	11 BORED	11 DEAR	11 DENTS	11 EIGHT
12 AIL	12 BUTT	12 CAPITAL	12 KOI	12 FLOUR

Page 35	Page 46	Page 47	Page 55	Page 56
1 FLU	1 GATE	1 HIRE	1 JEWEL	1 KOI
2 FINALLY	2 GOURD	2 HARE	2 JAM	2 NOSE
3 FACTS	3 GRAHAM	3 GRADE	3 NOT	3 NO
4 FEET	4 HOLE	4 IDLE	4 COLONEL	4 GENES
5 FOUL	5 HEAL	5 HORSE	5 KNIGHT	5 JEST
6 FEW	6 HOUR	6 HALL	6 KNOT	6 KARAT
7 EYES	7 INN	7 GUESSED	7 JOULE	7 COY
8 FIND	8 GRAM	8 AIR	8 JAMB	8 KNOCK
9 FRIAR	9 HEEL	9 HEAR	9 NIGHT	9 KNOWS
10 FAZED	10 OUR	10 GATOR	10 KERNEL	10 JEANS
11 FUR	11 IN	11 HAVE	11 NIGHT	11 CARROT
12 FLEA	12 WHOLE	12 HIGHER	12 NOT	12 KNOW

ANSWERS FROM THE DANGER TWINS

The Danger Twins have the answer keys!

Page 68

1 NEW
2 MOOSE
3 LYNX
4 NAVAL
5 MAIL
6 MAID
7 LEAK
8 LAY
9 MOUSSE
10 MALE
11 MADE
12 KNEW

Page 69

1 LAPS
2 MEET
3 LESSON
4 MIND
5 LIGHT
6 NONE
7 MIST
8 LOOT
9 NEED
10 LOCH
11 MADE
12 LOOSE

Page 83

1 WON
2 QUEUE
3 PLANE
4 PEAR
5 QUARTS
6 ROSE
7 RING
8 ROAD
9 OAR
10 PLAIN
11 PAIR
12 ROWS

Page 84

1 PIECE
2 RAIN
3 OVERDUE
4 READ
5 PASTE
6 ROLL
7 PAIL
8 POLE
9 PRINCE
10 RYE
11 POUR
12 ROUTE

Page 93

1 TOE
2 SON
3 TOO
4 SHOE
5 SAIL
6 TAIL
7 TOW
8 SUN
9 TWO
10 TALE
11 SALE
12 SHOO

Page 94

1 STEAK
2 TEA
3 TOAD
4 TEAR
5 SCENE
6 TENTS
7 SEA
8 TIED
9 CELLAR
10 TIGHTEN
11 SIGHED
12 TEASE

Page 111

1 WOOD
2 EARN
3 WITCH
4 ZERO
5 WHALE
6 AX
7 YOLK
8 UNREEL
9 WOULD
10 WHICH
11 VEIL
12 ZERO

Page 112

1 UNDO
2 WAR
3 VARY
4 WEIGH
5 WAVE
6 WORN
7 VIAL
8 WEAK
9 WASTE
10 WEE
11 WAIT
12 RIGHT

AMAZING BONUS MAZE FOR COMPLETING THIS BOOK!

This book was

completed by

THE DANGER TWINS

theDangerTwins.com